The Miracle

of a

Thank You

By

Cheri Staub

ISBN 1-4196-7834-5

Library of Congress Control Number: 2007908100
Publisher: BookSurge Publishing
North Charleston, South Carolina

Designed by Scott Mead

Dedication:

For my late husband Bill, who showed me what it is truly like to have a real family of unconditional love by bringing me into his. My eternal thank you for this miracle.

Acknowledgements:

First of all I must thank God for gifting me with faith and perseverance. Thank you Jesus for guiding me all the way and constantly reminding me "there is no separation"

I'd like to give a special thank you to Wendy Turkel and Scott and Debi Mead for believing in and encouraging me to follow through with publishing this little book. Plus a huge thank you for all of their computer help. I truly couldn't have completed it without them.

Another thank you to my son Jeff and his beautiful wife Leanna, for all their encouraging support and "advice" along with their unconditional love as well.

Then, I need to thank also my aunt Dolores, who has been my tower of strength from the day I was born.

Thank you all, I love you

Thank You

How can I tell you Thank You

Truly there are very many ways

Remind me daily to verbalize them

From the first morning light to

The dark days end

Let me never take you for granted

Nor forget that you honor my life

Let me always praise you with

A thank You

For remaining steadfast by my side

The miracle of a thank you

Can change a saddened heart

Because it conveys to the giver

Appreciation for their part

Thank You in:

Abenaki   Maine, USA, Montreal

Canada........Wliwni ni

Achuar Equador, Peru

............Yuuminsame

The miracle of a thank you

Can brighten any face

With a smile that too says to the giver

Their time was well spent

And their actions worthwhile

Afrikaans   South Africa

............Dankie

Akha China, Southeast asia

.......Gui lah hui mi a de

The miracle of a thank you

Can surprise an offending foe

Stopping a rage in mid sentence

Changing his anger to a peaceful glow

Alabamu Texas, USA

.... Kanobi

Albanian Albania, Yugoslavia

.... Faleminderit

The miracle of a thank you

Is sure to every time,

Make a person happy

With a desire to be just and kind

Ambo Angola, Namibia

...Ondapandula unene

Apache Arizona, USA

.........Asoge

The miracle of a thank you

Shows your parents took the time

To teach you that a thank you breaks down

Barriers of all kinds

Arabic Middle East, N. Africa

........Shukran

Arabic Morocco Praise to Allah

.......El-hamdullah

The miracle of a thank you

Shows especially to me

That love and appreciation

is truly all we need

Armenian   Western Armenia

......Shad shenorhagal em

Assyrian   Eastern Assrian

by plural...Basimeh

The miracle of a thank you

Shows consideration for another

Brings to the surface feelings that

We certainly are all brothers

Aymara' Bolivia, Peru, Chile
.... Juspajarana

Aymara' Bolivia, Peru, Chile
.......Dios pagaraka'tam

The miracle of a thank you

Shows these two words can

Tend and mend.

Also strengthen the bonds of

Love between friends

Azerbaijani Azerbaijan, Iran

......Taeshaekkur Elaeyiraem

Balinese Bali

......Matu suksama

The miracle of a thank you

Shows in a family of love and trust

Certainly a simple little thank you

Tends to mean so much

Bashkir Russia

... Rekhmet

Basque Navarrese Spain

..... Esker mila

The miracle of a thank you

Shows for all human kind respect

Plus a feeling of pride within oneself

For the actions of cause and effect

Belorussian Belarus

....Dzia'kuj

Bislama Vanuatu

....Tangkiu

The miracle of a thank you

Shows you're well aware and know

The energy you give out

Is exactly what you will be shown

Breton Brittany France

..... Trugarez

Bukusu Mt.Elgon, Kenya

..... Webaale

The miracle of a thank you

Shows love and gratitude

Can change a tear into a smile

And brighten any mood

Burmese   Myanmar

...Chezu tinbade

Burushashki   Northern Pakistan

......Bakhshish

The miracle of a thank you

Can on a cloudy afternoon:

Chase all the clouds away and

Make you whistle a happy tune

Cantonese Chinese China

.... Doh je

Cassubian Northwest Poland old

...... Bo'g zaplac

The miracle of a thank you

Can and most likely will

Suggest to the world that a thank you

Is better than a happy pill

Chamorro Guam

.....Si yu'os ma'ase'

Cheyenne United States

.....Ne'a' 'eshe

The miracle of a thank you

Can draw from the heart

The memory of a past event where a

Thank you played a major part

Chinook Jargon North America

.......Masiem

Chitonga Malawi

....Yewo

The miracle of a thank you

If you stop to think

Takes not one bit longer

Than for an eye to blink

Choctaw Oklahoma, U.S.

.... Yokoke

Chuukes Micronesia

.... Kili so

The miracle of a thank you

Shows they are easy words to say

Flowing more and more easily if you

Say them day to day

Chuvash Russia

..... Tavssi

Cornish Great Briton – Modern

..... Durdaladawhy

The miracle of a thank you

If taught from early birth

Could nurture a new generation

Restoring peace again to earth

Corsican France

......A ringrazie vi

Cree Canada

...... Mikwec

The miracle of a thank you

Flows easily from the lips

If it's said often enough

Through the entire body it wicks

Croatian Bosnia, Yugoslavia very much

..............Hvala

Croation Bosnia, Yugoslavia very much

........Puno hvala

The miracle of a thank you

Means recognizing another's gifts

Be it a present, maybe a helping hand

A kind thought that gives you a lift

Dakota North America

......Pidamayado

Dega Vietnam

.......Lac jak

The miracle of a thank you

Means acknowledging another's needs

And knowing at this moment in time

Your planting healing seeds

Dekelh Carrier Canada very much

...... Musicho

Dekelh Lheidli Canada by 3 to 1

.... Nenachailya

The miracle of a thank you

Like a candle burning bright

Emits a glow from its aura

Spreading warmth along with it's light

Deklh Nak'albun Canada by 2 to 1

..... Nenachailya

Dhivehi Maldives very much

.... Vara bodah shukriyyaa

The miracle of a thank you

Can project itself in seconds

Thousands of miles away,

Bringing the past to the very present

Dutch Netherlands, Belgin informal

.......Dankje

Egyptian Ancient Egypt to a woman

.......Dua Netjer en et i

The miracle of a thank you

Can humble any man

Therefore leveling the communication field

Giving mankind a helping hand

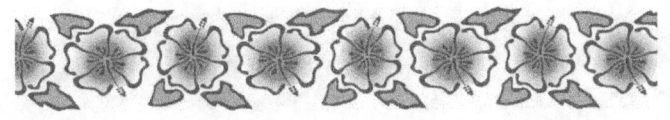

English America   informal

...... Thanks

English Old English old Britian sing

......Ic pancie pe

The miracle of a thank you

Is like money in the bank

An investment in your future

Insuring to elevate relationships

To a higher rank

Eton Cameroon

.....Abumgang

Faroese Faroe islands

......Takk fyri

The miracle of a thank you

Has a absolutely shown

Much better communication

When introduced into your home

Figian Fiji

..... Vinaka

Frisian Westerlauwer Netherlands

...... Tanke wol

The miracle of a thank you

Will play upon your mind

The many other thank yous

Throughout all of time

Gallo France

.... Merczi

German Central Europe

.... Danke

The miracle of a thank you

Begets the same respect

From any and all nationalities

Allowing any differences to accept

German Switzerland in spoken

.........Dank schon

Greek Greece, Cyprus very much

....Efharisto poli

The miracle of a thank you

Has been around for quite some time

Eons and eons of years before

Blessing all of mankind

Gumatj Australia

.........Ga

Gurung Nepal to an equal or superior

.....Dxanyaa'baad

The miracle of a thank you

Shows no exception to the rule

That if applied more frequently

Is a very hand tool

Gwich'in Alaska

.....Mahsi ` choo

Han Alaska

.....Mahsi´

The miracle of a thank you

Can create heaven here on earth

Instilling in every individual

A feeling of incredible worth

Hawaiian Hawaii

......Mahalo

Hindi   India, East Asia, Surname

......Danyavad

The miracle of a thank you

When coupled with a please

Is sure to show the listener

This person will always succeed

Hmong Njua Northern Thailand

.....Zoo sab muab

Hope North America said by women

...... Heve'

The miracle of a thank you

Even to the very rudest

Will always shield you from another's

Harsh words

Protection that's the truest

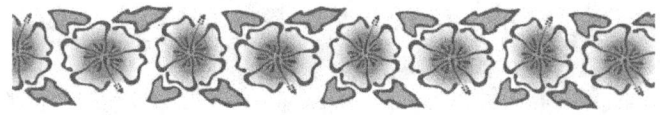

Huave Mexico

.....Dios manguy ic

Hungarian Magyar Hungary

.......Koszi

The miracle of a thank you

Not only helps yourself

But adds so much to the unified field

Somewhere out there it is felt

Icelandic Iceland

........Takk

Igbo Ibo Nigeria

.....Yauwa'

The miracle of a thank you

While taking less time than a minute to say

Can often stay with you

Throughout the entire day

Ilokano Philippines   very much

......Agyamanac unay

Ingush Russia in spoken language

......Barkl

The miracle of a thank you

Speaks of a higher nature

That heals the soul within the heart

And honors our true maker

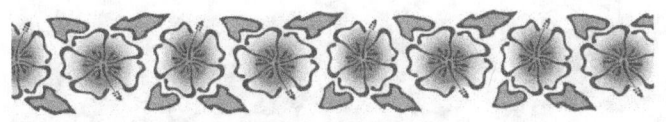

Innu Labrador and Quebec Canada

..... Tshinashkumitan

Inuktitut Canada

..... Nakorami

The miracle of a thank you

Bespeaks of a kinder mind

One that cares to preserve and save

The world from a negative time

Irish Gaelic Ireland to more than one

........Go raibh maith agaibh

Itbayaten Batanes Philippines

.....Ah Dios mamexes

The miracle of a thank you

Can restore ones destructive thoughts

Encouraging a transformation

Something that cannot be bought

Itzaj Itza' Maya Guatemala

...D'yos b'otik

Japanese Japan

...Domo arigato

The miracle of a thank you

Teaches us over and over again

It really is important to be aware

Of the message being sent

Japanese Tohoku Ben North East Japan

......Oshoshina

Jerriais Jersey

....Merci bein des fais

The miracle of a thank you

The moment it is heard

Allows the listener the readiness

To hear another word

Kachin Burma

.....Chyeju gaba sai

Kannada India

.....Vandane

The miracle of a thank you

Prepares the situation

To flourish without a hindrance

Providing comfort and elation

Karen Thailand

.......Da blu

Kashmiri India, Pakistan, China

.......Danawad

The miracle of a thank you

Makes it very easy to see

If we create happiness in our lives

That's exactly what we will be

Keres Southwestern United States

.........Khuu'a

Khowar Central Asia

......Mehrbani

The miracle of a thank you

Makes you feel like you can proceed

Carry on without a shred of doubt

It is in this moment we receive

Kiga Africa

.... Wabare

Kikongo Congo, Angola, Cuba

.... Wuanka

The miracle of a thank you

Truly heavens words

If one is truly honest

They'll admit they are happy to be heard

Kingarwanda Rwamda, Congo-kinshasa inf

.... Urakoze

Kiswahili Southeast Africa

.....Aksante

The miracle of a thank you

Shows that when a rogue is ready to turn

Often it is a thank you

That gave him his concerns

Klallam Washington, USA   to a friend

....Ha?neng cen, nascha?che

Kohistani Central Asia

.....Shukria

The miracle of a thank you

Shows that from the heart

Humility and love

Certainly were the first to impart

Korean Korea

.... Komapsumnida

Krio Sierra Leone

.... Tenkey

The miracle of a thank you

I'm sure you'll all agree

Often will cause someone to overhear

And smile at the one who speaks

Kurdi   Middle East

......Sipas dikim

Kwe'yol Haiti thank you very muvh

.......Mesi plen

The miracle of a thank you

Is music to the ears

That one will remember long after the song

For years and year and years

Ladin Badia Valley Italy

.....Dilan

Ladino Spain

.........Muchas Gracias

The miracle of a thank you

Time after time after time

Instills the very likeness of living

Life to the sublime

Lakota N. America very much

.......Pilamaya aloh

Latin Ancient Rome, Vatican

.......Gratias

The miracle of a thank you

If you still have any doubt

Will restore to you your faith and

Into the ethers hurrah!, you will shout

Lenape Deleware United States

.... Wanishi

Lingua Franca Mediterranean very much

.... Mouchou gratzia

The miracle of a thank you

In case you still don't know

Brings you so much closer

To the essence of your soul

Lithuanian Lithuania Very much
........Labai achiu

Low Saxon Eastern Friesland, Germany
......Dank

The miracle of a thank you

Morning noon or night

Can be the intercession and

Spare you from your plight

Luganda Uganda

.... Webale

Lunyoro West Uganda

.... Webale

The miracle of a thank you

Even if you sound hysterical

Brings about blessings you've never thought of

That appear to be quite ethereal

Luxembourgish Luxembourg

.......Merci

Mabuiag Australia

.........Eso

The miracle of a thank you

Brings peace to the hopeful

And causes them to think

You are extremely thoughtful

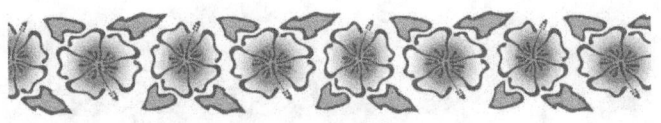

Malagasy   Madagascar formal
...... Misaotra tompoko

Mam   Guatemala
.... Chjoonta

The miracle of a thank you

Can and always will

Add dimensions to an adventure

Making it even better still

Mandarin Chinese, China

.......Xie Xie

Maori New Zealand

.... Tika hoki

The miracle of a thank you

Can linger in your heart

Soon you'll become acutely aware

There is no separation, not even from the start

Mapuche   Araucano South America

.....Chaltu

Marshallese   Marshall Islands

...... Kommol

The miracle of a thank you

Spoken in any language

Can alleviate your fear and

Eliminate your anguish

Mazatec Mexico

Nkhi k'a ninashitechino

Mikmig Canada

..... Wela'lin

The miracle of a thank you

With just the hint of an accent in fact

Can tickle your funny bone and

Remind you that you are all that

Mixtec Oaxaca Mexico family

.... Ku'ta' uri

Mixtec Magdalena Penasco Oaxaco

Mexico

..........Cacutahvixensa

The miracle of a thank you

Will settle down a nervous state

Even if it is long overdue

Or just a little bit late

Mohican North America

.......Oneowe

Mongolian Mongolia, N. China

...............Bayarlalaa

The miracle of a thank you

If you take a closer look

Can show an untrained eye

The spreading of this message and

Just how long it took

Moore' Mossi Burkina Faso

.......Barka

Morisyen Mauritius

.......Mersi

The miracle of a thank you

Sounds gentle to your ears

Words so very peaceful

Sometimes bring fourth happy tears

Muskogee Oklahoma and Florida USA

.......Henka

Na'huatl Tepoztlan Mexico

.......Tlazocamati

The miracle of a thank you

While we're on the subject

Can dance you around the dictionary

For words to compare it with magic

Nandi Kenya

.......Asai

Navajo United States

.......Ahe'hee'

The miracle of a thank you

Like magic is very rare

However, the return of it's usage

Could cause it to flourish

And prosper everywhere

Ndebele Zimbabwe very much

.... Ngeyabonga Kakulu

Ndjuka Suriname

......A bigi ba

The miracle of a thank you

Once again becoming heard

Makes any language sound more sweet

And you'll savor every word

Nganasan Russia

.... Nage

Niuean Nieu south pacific very much

....Fakaaue lahi mahaki

The miracle of a thank you

Helps the trials of every day life

Softens the blows of society

Bringing you to new heights

Norwegian Sorftlandsk Sortland Norway

......Takk

Ojibwe Chippewa, Anishinaabe No,

America0

.....Miigwech

The miracle of a thank you

When you're feeling all your woes

Can surely change the way you feel

Making you smile from your head to your toes

Oromo Kenya, Somalia

..... Maharaba

Paamese Vanuatu

...... Namasmasuk

The miracle of a thank you

Always stops to make you think

If a thank you can make you feel this good

On a global scale, what could it bring

Palauan Palau

......Sulang

Pende Congo-Kinshasa

.....Hambadiahana

The miracle of a thank you

In times that you may quarry

Will always pull you through

Even though you may tarry

Pohnpeian Micronesia

...... Kalangan

Polish Poland familiar

.... Dzieki

The miracle of a thank you

Does actually invoke

The wishes of the universe

As the angels words bespoke

Potawatomi United States

.....Iwgwien

Provencal Occitan, France

......Merce'

The miracle of a thank you

Can stop a lonely tear

From staining the face of sadness

Bringing back gladness that's always near

Punjabi India

.......Shukria

Quechua Ayacuchano Peru

.........Diyus papapusonga

The miracle of a thank you
When your life seems really dull
Can give you a different outlook
You'll know then the glass is half full

Quechua Cochabambino Cochabamba Bolivia

.......Pachis

Quechua Cuzqueno Cuzco Peru

....Grasias

The miracle of a thank you

You'll find out over time

Only increases in value

A rewarding fact you will find

Quichua Equador

......Diusulupagui

Romani Romany Gypsy Europe

.....Gestena

The miracle of a thank you

Tends to make it so

That many; many more miracles

Happen wherever you go

Romansch Switzerland

....Grazia

Rotuman Pacific Islands

....Noa'ia

The miracle of a thank you

Will beyond all your days

Always be enlightening

In very many ways

Saami Lappish Scandinavia very much

.......Giitus eanat

Saanich Vancouver Island Canada

..........Hay sxw q'a

The miracles of a thank you

Will someday show the world

A great healing will come from these two

words

That are as precious as a beautiful pearl

Samoan Samoa thank you very much

....Fa'afetai tele

Sarnami Suriname, Holland

......Sukriya

The miracle of a thank you

Has to me, become very clear

And the miracle of unity I know

Is absolutely near

Scottish Gaelic   Scotland

......Tapadh leibh

Scots Ulster scots Northern Ireland

.....Tenks

The miracle of a thank you

Has shown that it can bring

Wonders yet to make up happy and

Many a wondrous thing

Sepedi South Africa

..... Ke a leboga

Serrere Sengal, Gambia

..... Dioka ndjiale

The miracle of a thank you

Shows you how it goes

Whenever you employ a thank you

How a happy spirit grows

Setswana Botswana, So. Africa

..........Ke itumela

Sgaw Karen Thailand

.....Dah bluet

The miracle of a thank you

If coming from a dog will get you

The wag of a tail or lick of a tongue

Then lies down by your feet, like a bump on a

log

Sherpa Helambu Nepal, Tibet

.... Thuchi chea

Sicilian Sicily Italy

.... Grazzii

The miracle of a thank you

If coming from a cat

Will bring you instant purring

While curled up on your lap

Siswati Swazi Swaziland by one person

.... Ngiyabonga

Slovenian Slovania very much

.... Havala lepa

The miracle of a thank you

If really sincerely felt

Will give you a winning hand

When all the cards are dealt

Spanish Spain, America

.....Gracias

Sudovian Baltic Region

.....Denka

The miracle of a thank you

Begets laughter from the soul

That merges with the universal

And gladdens the world as a whole

Suryoyo Syria Turkey

.... Tawdi

Swedish Sweden, Finland

.... Tack sa' mycket

The miracle of a thank you

Has s systemic effect

And the little rewards accumulate

Like building blocks of success

Tagalog Philippines   very much

.........Maraming salamat

Tahitian Tahiti

..........Mauruuru roa

The miracle of a thank you

Never, ever ends

Just continues on forever

Through the universe of friends

Tamashek Tamahog, Tuareg West Africa

...   .Tanumert

Tanana   Alaska

.......Basee choo

The miracle of a thank you

May sometimes go unnoticed

But the effects can be felt subliminally

Like breathing the scent of a beautiful lotus

Telugu India

....Dhanyavaadaalu

Tetum E. Timor by a woman

..........Obrigada

The miracle of a thank you

Is a universal thought

Portraying the admiration of

Gratefulness artfully taught

Tewa Southeastern United States

............kuunda

Thai Thailand very much

.........Khawp khun makh

The miracle of a thank you

Yields a feeling of worthiness

That transcends race or gender

To show that we are all blessed

Tigrinya Ethiopia, Eritrea

.... Yekanyelay

Tlingit Canada, Alaska very much

.... Atlein gunalche'esh

The miracle of a thank you

Can turn a frown into a smile

To ease the pressures of the days

Sometimes arduous trials

Tongan Tonga, So. Pacific Island
.... Malo

Tschiluba Kasai oc. Reg., Congo-Kinsakadila
.... Twasakadila

The miracle of a thank you

Paints a picture of good will

The more that it is used

Makes the picture even brighter still

Tupi Tembe´ Teneta'har Brizil by men

.......Azeharmo kui

Turkish Turkey N. Cypress

........Tesekkur ederim

The miracle of a thank you

Is no more, nor less

One of the greatest miracles

That all men surely can attest

Turkish Turkey N. Cypress very much

....Cok tesekkur ederim

Tuscarora Southern Band USA. N.

Carolina

.......Nyeahweh

The miracle of a thank you

Along with "I love you" when said

Should be the last words uttered every night

When retiring to bed

Tzotzil Chiapas Mexico

.... Kolaval

Uchinaaguchi Okinawa Japan

.... Nihci deebiru

The miracle of a thank you

Allows the energy to flow

So that generation after generation

Great peace they'll come to know

Ukranian Ukrain

.......Spasibi

Ute Colorado and Utah, USA

.... Togʼoyak

The miracle of a thank you

Nips sadness in the bud

It works especially well

When accompanied by a hug

Uyghur Central Asia

.... Rakhmat

Venda South Africa

.... Ndi a livhuha

The miracle of a thank you

When practiced every day

Makes the world seem sweeter

And chases all the clouds away

Vietnamese Vietnam

...Cám ơn

Visayan Cebuano, Philippines

....Salamat

The miracle of a thank you

Especially among friends

Will always insure that friendship

No matter how much life buckles and bends

Votic Russia

......Passibo

Walloon Belgium

...... Merci

The miracle of a thank you

Can always bring to us hope

For the entire world around us

So no longer we'll see people mope

Welsh Wales formal

....Diolch yn fawr

Wintu California, USA

...cala da mat doyut

The miracle of a thank you

Even when you're feeling blue

Will keep the energy flowing,

Helping even you

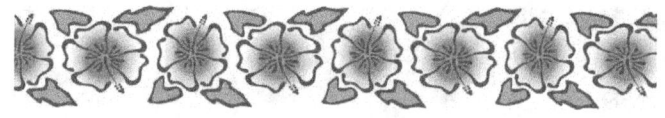

Xhosa South Africa

......Enkosi

Yaka Angola, Congo-Kinshasa

...... Koloombo

The miracle of a thank you

Will bring about much praise

So everyone can live a better life

With the happiest of days

Yoruba Nigeia

.....Oshe

Yucatec Yucatan Mexico

.........Dios bo'otik

The miracle of a thank you

May seem very small

But added to love and gratitude

They're the grandest words of all

Yuki United States

.. Mis tatk

Yolngu Matha Australia

..... Yo manymak

The miracle of a thank you

Gives you strength and power

To always hold your head up high

And never have to cower

Yup'ik Siberia

.....Quyanaghhalek

Zapotec Yatzach Mexico

........Choshcwlentio'

The miracle of a thank you

Can spice your life with fun

So everyone will know enjoyment

When all is said and done

Zarma Dyerma W. Africa
.... Fofo

Zulu South Africa, Lesotho
.... Ngiyabonga

With love and gratitude

and

Peace to the world

I now

Thank you